B

BRE

EBERHARD
ARNOLD

EBERHARD ARNOLD

EBERHARD ARNOLD

A TESTIMONY OF CHURCH COMMUNITY FROM HIS LIFE AND WRITINGS

PLOUGH PUBLISHING HOUSE

 Rifton, New York

© 1964, 1973 by the Plough Publishing House of
The Woodcrest Service Committee, Inc.
Rifton, New York

Originally published in England as the Autumn
1953 issue of *The Plough* to commemorate the
70th anniversary of Eberhard Arnold's birth

Handbound edition published in the U.S.A. in
1964, with selections added

This new edition published in 1973, reset
in a new format with added illustrations,
to commemorate the 90th anniversary of
Eberhard Arnold's birth

ISBN 0-87486-112-8
Library of Congress Catalog Card Number:
73-11605
Printed at the Plough Press, Farmington, Pa., U.S.A.

CONTENTS

THE ALM BRUDERHOF IN LIECHTENSTEIN

THE RHÖN BRUDERHOF IN GERMAN

INTRODUCTION

The little stable in Bethlehem was the place where God's love broke in. And the mysterious men who came from the land of the rising sun followed the star and discovered the place where the secret of love was laid in the manger of the animals, wrapped in swaddling clothes, in the helplessness of a human baby. They discovered the place where God's love broke in.

This is the most important thing for every man, that in his time, at his hour, he discovers the breaking in of God's love, and that then he follows the star which has fallen into his heart. Let King Herod come then, with his threats, and drive those who follow the star and who come to the star of love, from the country, indeed drive the divine Child himself out of the country—it means nothing for those who follow the star.

> And the angel of the Lord will protect
> the revelation of love in the midst of times
> of the greatest hatred and of the heaviest
> darkness which has spread over the earth.
> *Eberhard Arnold*

With this witness to the power of God's love, we want to introduce this little volume. We bring it out on the eightieth anniversary of Eberhard's birth, glad to be able to share these words by him, by his wife Emmy, and by his friends. Eberhard is our beloved brother, and we hope that through this book many more can become acquainted with him.

In these recent years especially, we have seen again and again how we hinder and oppose that very love we long to serve and that Eberhard served. It is an overwhelming and tender witness to the wonderful mystery of unity, that in just this recognition that we are a hindrance to God's love, we have felt closer to Eberhard himself and to the life and the Spirit to which he gave his life as witness. As his witness comes alive for us, we long to share it with others.

> The brothers and sisters
> of the Bruderhof communities
> Christmas 1963

FIRE SONG

Radiance descend! Radiance descend!
Thou, Sun of all love eternal,
Let every impulse infernal
Sink to the grave! Sink to the grave!

Fire consume! Fire consume!
All that to Death is given,
All that with envy is riven,
Fire consume! Fire consume!

Light of the Heights! Light of the Heights!
Sun of all-glowing rays and brightness,
Stars in unnumbered, countless lightness,
Light of the Heights! Light of the Heights!

Break to us now! Break to us now!
Power of eternal radiance glowing,
Pour forth in flaming flood o'erflowing,
Surrender now! Surrender now!

Radiance on high! Radiance on high!
Thou resurrected life, giving
To us eternal power living.
Radiance on high! Radiance on high!

Strahle herab!
Eberhard and Emmy Arnold
Easter 1926

RHÖN DINING ROOM

RHÖN CHILDREN'S HOUSE

EBERHARD LEADING TOUR OF FARM AT THE RHÖN

WHITSUN CONFERENCE AT SANNERZ, 1920

EBERHARD SHARING LETTERS

EBERHARD ARNOLD'S
LIFE AND WORK

by EMMY ARNOLD

Eberhard Arnold was born in Königsberg on the 26th of July 1883. He was the third son of Carl Franklin Arnold, who was a high school teacher at the time. His mother, Elizabeth Arnold, née Voigt, came from an old family of scholars. His paternal grandfather, Franklin Luther Arnold, was a missionary of English and American descent, and pastor of a Presbyterian Church in the United States.

Eberhard had a brother and three sisters. When he was five, the family left Königsberg, since his father had been called to Breslau as professor of Church history. Eberhard was full of wild ideas and boyish pranks which left him little time for school. Because of all his mischief, he was not always in the good graces of his teachers and his classmates' parents. Even as a

child he objected to social inequality and made
friends with the very poor and with tramps. He
found more warm-heartedness and genuine humanity in them than in middle-class people.
Once on vacation he was staying at his uncle's
country parsonage. He was strongly impressed
by the inward religious warmth of this man,
particularly because he took the part of the poor
and oppressed, which aroused the hostility of
the rich members of his congregation. It was in
his uncle's house that he first met a member of
the Salvation Army. The brotherly way in which
his uncle spoke with this man while Eberhard
was there was a powerful impulse to him in the
direction of a genuine Christian love, which
shows its strength precisely in love of the very
poor. So Eberhard, then sixteen years old, experi-
enced a radical inner change. He told his parents
and teachers that his life was going to take a
completely different direction from then on, but
they did not understand him.

In his search for people of kindred spirit,
Eberhard made connection with a number of
groups that had been stirred by Christ. A group
of other students gathered around him, seeking
through Bible study to find a deeper realization

of the way of Jesus. The Salvation Army had made a great impression on him. He went with these devoted people into the darkest haunts of Breslau in the urge to free men from drink and filth. He went with one heavy drinker to and from work every morning and evening, because the way went past a bar. Profoundly shocked by the misery of the poor in Breslau's East End, he found the social life of his middle-class parents increasingly hard to endure. Thinking of the misery of the poor, he refused to attend a certain social function because he found it wrong to spend so much money in one evening to entertain the well-to-do, whereupon his father confined him to his room. His parents by no means consented to his new activities, and certainly not to his attitude on the social question.

When Eberhard had finished school, his parents insisted that he study theology, although his own opinion was that he could be of more service to men as a doctor. In Breslau, Halle, and Erlangen, he studied theology, philosophy, and educational method, concluding his years at the university with a doctoral dissertation on *Early Christian and Antichristian Elements in the Development of Friederich Nietzsche*. While

EBERHARD AND EMMY ARNOLD

SANNERZ   WHITSUN 1920

he was in Halle he became intimately connected with the German Student Christian Movement, and worked for several years in close cooperation with Ludwig von Gerdtell. Both of them worked in the midst of the revivalist movement which was stirring so many spiritual seekers at the time.

It was during this time, in 1907, that we met. After some profound and earnest talks together about the nature of Christian discipleship, we were engaged, though we had known each other only a few days. From then on, we went our way together. We were married in 1909. During the first years of our marriage, Eberhard was much sought-after as a lecturer. He spoke in various German cities, such as Halle, Leipzig, Berlin, Dresden, and Hamburg about the crucial problems of the time. Some of his subjects were "Early Christianity in the Present Day," "Social Distress," "Freedom for Every Man," "The Distress and Enslavement of the Masses," "Present-Day Religious Struggles," "Jesus as He Really Was," and "Nietzsche's Criticism of Christianity."

It was then that Eberhard's conflict with the State Church began, brought on chiefly by the question of baptism. Eberhard saw that the

Church was on the wrong foundation because of its connections with the State and with property. This realization made a decisive difference to our lives. Eberhard was baptized and left the State Church. He consequently could not accept a post in it. Stimulated by the writings of the Swiss religious-socialist pastor Hermann Kutter, he increasingly took the part of the proletariat and all other oppressed classes. His declared attitude to the working class and to the State Church resulted in numerous disputes with his parents and with the Church authorities.

In 1913 Eberhard contracted a serious illness of the lungs and larynx, and therefore our little family moved to the southern Tyrol, where we were able to rent a cottage near Bozen. This time gave us the opportunity for thorough meditation which led to deeper clarity. It was then that Eberhard wrote the first chapters of the book *Innenland* and a series of important essays, such as "Love to Christ," "Love to the Brothers," and "The Power of the Life of Prayer." He also made a thorough study of Anabaptist history; and figures like Hans Denck, Balthasar Hubmaier, and Thomas Münzer made a great impression on us during these months. At this time, it became increasingly clear to us that our life had to take a more radical and active direction. From this time onward, my sister Else von Hollander lived with us, and took a very lively share in everything that concerned us. While I was very much taken up with nursing Eberhard and caring for the children, she helped him in his scholarly work as his secretary. She was one of those who began to live in community with us, and after that was of great help to Eberhard until her death in 1932.

The First World War broke out in 1914, while we were in the midst of these inner experiences. Eberhard was drafted into the army and served for several weeks as a driver in the Service Corps in eastern Germany. He was soon discharged because of his poor health. From then on he was constantly preoccupied by the military question, though it took some time for him to arrive at a clear solution.

Then we lived in Halle for a while, until 1915, when Eberhard was called to Berlin as literary director of the *Furche-Verlag* (Furrow Publishing House). Our family stayed in Berlin until 1920. Besides its periodical, *Die Furche*, the publishing house issued a series of books

and art-folios for the use of prisoners of war.
Eberhard was severely shocked by his frequent
visits to hospitals, and he grew increasingly
opposed to the war spirit.

After 1919 we found a current of new life
coming to us from all sides. At Whitsun that
year Eberhard spoke in Marburg to members of
the German Student Christian Movement. Jesus'
words came alive for the people at this meeting, showing us in the Sermon on the Mount
the perfectly clear solution to the problems of
war and social injustice.

Erwin Wissman, in reporting on this Whitsun
conference in *Die Furche*, wrote: "The focus
of all that was said and thought was Jesus'
Sermon on the Mount. Eberhard Arnold burned
it into our hearts with passionate spirituality,
hammered it into our wills with prophetic power
and the tremendous mobile force of his whole
personality. This was the Sermon on the Mount
in the full force of its impact, in its absolute
and undiminished relevance, its unconditional
absoluteness. Here there was no compromise.
Whoever wants to belong to this Kingdom, must
give himself wholly and go through with it to

the last! To be a Christian means to live the life of Christ. We are obligated by a burning challenge: the rousing summons to love, and the ominous, 'He that takes the sword shall perish by the sword.' The beginnings of a decisive spiritual revolution depend upon us . . . it is up to us to do the deeds of Jesus in His Spirit, to help men in body, in soul and spirit. This is the only way we Christians can follow today as envoys of the Kingdom of God and as the vanguard of the only politics that is possible and necessary—the politics of Christocracy."

This Marburg conference was the beginning. It was here that we saw the vision of future things. The fruits of this experience became more and more apparent, until out of the vision life itself gradually assumed a new form.

It began with discussions, when we held open house in Berlin. Often as many as eighty or a hundred came, people from the most various groupings of opinion—members of the Youth Movement, workers, students, atheists, evangelicals, anarchists, Quakers. The question burning in us all was, "What shall we do?" The discussion centered around the Sermon on the Mount.

Everyone knew that life had to be changed.
There had to be action at last! No more words!
We want to see action!

This radical attitude led to controversy with
the directors of *Die Furche* and the German
Student Christian Movement. In various conferences like those in Bad Oeyenhausen and at
Saarow, the struggle went on over crucial questions such as: "What is the Christian's attitude
to war and revolution?" and, "Can a Christian be
a soldier?" Eberhard's answer was an emphatic
"No."

A report on these conferences says: "Eberhard
Arnold was glad to admit the necessity of personal rebirth, but said that the ethic of Jesus
should be part of every evangelization. Jesus did
recognize the power of the State, but character-
ized the Kingdom of God as something entirely
different. The Christian represents a continual
corrective within the State, an arousing of conscience and a strengthening of the will of justice,
a leaven, that is, a foreign body in the sense of
a higher value. But insofar as the State uses
force, the Christian must refuse to cooperate.
Hence he cannot be a soldier, executioner, or
policeman. It is our duty to testify in word and

action that nothing in the words of Jesus may be distorted. The demand is always absolute: 'We must obey God rather than men.' We feel we are in the world as a corrective to the norm."

Now new ways had to be found and taken. We answered the call of the friends of the "New Work," a group of religious socialists, and the summons to the "original Church" that reached us from Schlüchtern. First we and some of our friends proposed a Whitsuntide conference in Schlüchtern. About two hundred people, most of them young, came from all parts of Germany with the urge to find an answer to the burning question, "What shall we do?" How can we find true humanity, true freedom, and a genuinely dedicated life? Under the stimulus of a visit to the Free German Youth settlement, Habertshof, we realized that our way would have to be one of brotherly community life. We regarded private property and possessions as one of the most evil roots of war and all the wrongness of human life.

But where to begin? In the city, or in the country? What is the best way to relieve the misery of the masses? The answer our working-class friends gave was, "Go into the country."

From the start, it was clear to us that community life would have to be a life of unity in faith, and of community of property and work in voluntary poverty. Particularly the writings of Gustav Landauer turned us in this direction.

In the summer of 1920 we rented three small rooms at the back of an inn in the village of Sannerz, Kreis Schlüchtern. Nobody was thinking of starting a community with a new philosophy of life; we only wanted to put into practice, together with all who wanted to come and help, the things that had become clear to us. At the time we were only seven adults and five children. From the very outset the little group was sought out by many guests who so often arrived unexpectedly that we used to repeat the lines, "Ten were invited, twenty have come. Pour water in the soup, and bid all welcome."

We had many discussions with our guests, struggling for clarity about the questions that concerned us and them. These went on far into the night, but often after lively debate a powerful experience of fellowship was granted us.

Some extracts from a talk by Eberhard Arnold, "The Essence of our Development," give a good idea of what was begun in those days, not by human beings, and not willed in human strength by individuals. It was begun and established by the Spirit, and this is the only reason it has lasted.

"The important thing in the beginning of such a communal life is the inner situation, the inner atmosphere. The first period at Sannerz was surrounded by a flood of spiritual movement. There was a certain direction in the wind that filled the sails of the departing ships and blew them toward a specific destination. It was as though the stream of events had rushed in upon us from outside and was seeking its culmination and crystallization, its vortex of force, in our community life. It was possible for a person to spend a week with us at Sannerz without seeing the point of it all. But whoever really had the vision that saw into the depths and could look deep into men's hearts, inevitably realized that here there was a spiritual mission of the Gospel and the Church of Jesus Christ, a mission station right in the middle of a Germany, a central Europe, that was pagan and yet under the visitation of God. Among all of us, among those who came to us and those who were already there, the Holy Spirit brought about the mutuality of

our meeting before the face of God. The rooms
in Sannerz and at the Rhön Bruderhof in the
early days were filled by a power that did not
come from us who lived there, nor from those
who came to visit us; it was a power that came
from God and visited us. This power was an
invisible fluid surrounding us. So we could understand Pentecost as the rushing of the Spirit that
surrounded the waiting Church community with
its visitation. In this wonderful mystery, community came into being, for here no will or word
that was merely our own could assert itself,
neither the word of a so-called leader nor the
word of a so-called opposition. The voice comes
out of the cloud, and man is still. But this does
not at all mean that only those who confess
Christ, who declare that they are converted and
reborn Christians, are touched by the cloud.
Quite the contrary is the case. We have seen it
happen again and again that the hidden Christ
is revealed in men who insist they have no faith.
Christ visits all men, long before they have
found unity with Him. We sense that the light
of Christ comes to all men who are born into
this world."

In 1922 there were many changes. Many of

our friends turned back to the old life. They were disillusioned: they said that people today were too individualistic to be able to give themselves up to the extent of being capable of community living. We felt the same incapability in ourselves, but we had heard the challenge of community life so distinctly that, for all our apprehension, we were determined to go through with it. Only seven ventured to begin again; all the rest went away. Objectively, the chief reason for the separation was the issue of faith versus purely economic reasoning. In a talk with some of our guests later on, Eberhard said of this time of crisis and new beginning:

"When the call first came to us, we felt that the Spirit of Jesus Christ had driven us and charged us to live in full community, in communal solidarity, with an open door and a loving heart for all people. It was the Word of Jesus Christ, the reality of His life and the fact of His Spirit, that gave us the strength to start firmly and certainly on this way and to keep on though our steps were short and feeble. When we had traveled only a short way on this path, times came upon us that put this power to the test, hostile times of trial, when friends we knew well and whom we had grown to love deeply, suddenly reversed their position and became enemies of the way, because they had turned away from freedom and unity, because they wanted to go back again into ordinary middle-class life, to normal private life and their own pocketbook. At that time, the movement was led into bondage again through the middle-class influences of capitalism and its business and professional life.

"But though most of our friends left us, though whole groups had deserted the flag of unity and freedom, though well-meaning friends might earnestly advise us that the way of freedom and unity would lead us to a lonely and ineffectual end, that could not change anything. With our own children and those we had adopted, we had to push through toward the goal."

Materially speaking, the new beginning was just as hard as the original start two years previously. Full of gratitude and courage, though somewhat hesitant, we set to work. Now we were living in a larger house at Sannerz and the size and tasks of the community were growing slowly. An important part of our work during these years was publishing, together with the education of underprivileged children, who grew up with our own children. The farm and garden work developed gradually.

The place at Sannerz was soon too small and we looked around for something else. In 1926, with very little capital, we bought the Sparhof in the Fulda district, a very poor and worked-out farm. It took some time to complete the move until we were all together again there in 1927 and could proceed to build up our communal life. It was quite different when we had a place that belonged to the community entirely. We wanted everything we did to symbolize the divine and the evolving Church. The children's community as an integral part of the whole, the garden and farm, the building, the craftwork and publishing, as well as our work with guests and with the poor, could now be reestablished and expanded, as far as we had the ability and strength to do it.

The full responsibility for all practical and spiritual activity was borne by the brotherhood which assigned to various members certain specific aspects of the work. Eberhard's chief task

during those years was to stimulate, deepen, and
clarify the life of this "socio-educational community of work," as it was called, particularly
in thinking through the problems of the various
departments of work. Meanwhile the community
was constantly growing. Young people came and
devoted themselves and all their energies to the
cause and the tasks facing the whole community.
It was not long before they could take over the
responsibility of directing certain branches of
the work.

During these years we spent at Sannerz and
at the Rhön Bruderhof, Eberhard was also giving
lectures in various cities in Germany, Austria,
and Switzerland, and took an active part in conferences of the Youth Movement and of pacifist
and other groups. His book *Die ersten Christen
nach dem Tode der Apostel* ("The Early Christians After the Death of the Apostles") appeared
in 1926. It was an attempt to express the power
of the Spirit which had animated the early
Christian Church and which had played a fundamental part in the beginning of the Bruderhof
community. He dedicated the book to his parents, grateful, in spite of the many disagreements
and struggles he had had with them, for the

influences of his home and for the growing understanding they showed as time went on for the life we had chosen.

Eberhard took a special interest in the care and education of the children, having a profound reverence for them and a realization that adults have much to learn from them. As a teacher, he knew how to arouse a lively interest in the children for the past and present history of mankind and in man's hopes for the future. Both old and young took part in the work on the land, particularly in sowing and harvest time. There was plenty of work to do and the times when the whole household worked together were an important part of the communal experience, for us and for our guests. The day was spent in work and the evening in discussions in which either the whole household or only the brotherhood took part. We went on hikes together and tried to find contact with the neighboring peasant-farmers. We used to sit under the village lime tree, singing and playing folksongs. Eberhard would read a story or legend, the peasants brought us something to eat and were drawn into our common experience. Occasionally we gave plays in the neighboring villages and tried to present a simple message. Or else we took long walks by starlight and gathered in the vaulted cellar of the Steckelsburg, the ancestral castle of Ulrich von Hutten, and sat around a roaring fire while Eberhard told us of Hutten's times: "It is a delight to be alive, the spirits are awaking!..." Then home again in the darkness.

Since the group kept growing we were always busy building, and mostly without enough funds. Eberhard was extremely interested in the planning of the houses. We wanted them to express the spirit that inspired us, with its characteristic simplicity. All took part in determining the way we built. Modesty and simplicity, but bright colors, like God's creation in all its diversity— that was what we wanted in our houses.

Another thing we always laid great stress on was craftwork, especially artistic crafts. The design for every candlestick or bowl that our wood-turning shop intended to make was communally appraised and decided. Eberhard always said that precisely this kind of work, in its simplicity of form, should testify to the way we felt as a community.

We later added a printing shop to our publishing house. Eberhard emphasized the beauty of the printed page and the neat execution of setting, printing, and binding. The producing of each book or article, even of some letters, was a matter that concerned the whole community. During communal work, for instance sorting out the potatoes, manuscripts were discussed and proof sheets read. In this way the members of the community gained a thorough knowledge of the books of our "Source" series, such as *The Early Christians, Francis of Assisi, Novalis, Zinzendorf,* and of other publications like the book *Innenland* which we revised.

In the mornings we met for a silent meeting. Our common mealtimes were a symbol for us of the coming Kingdom of justice, love, and peace. Our food was always simple, often poor, but we ate it from our earthenware bowls in an atmosphere of devotional fellowship in the well-lit dining room with its panelled walls, its green tables covered with red linoleum, and its seven-armed candlestick in the center.

On summer evenings we often gathered under the big beech tree on the hill overlooking the community. Here, with our guests and those who were working with us, we sought for the true inner liberation of the individual from himself, for true peace and the just society. This often developed into an earnest discussion of the kind of life that rises from the power of the love of Jesus. We repeatedly won through to a genuine experience of fellowship which led many who were there to a commitment of their whole lives.

In our meetings Eberhard strove to give us a vital appreciation of the most important spiritual movements of history. For example, we all studied the rise of Quakerism and the Anabaptist movement of the sixteenth century, giving special attention to the origins of the Hutterian communities in Moravia. We sensed that the same spirit that had led us together had been at work in this movement. Knowledge of the thousands of martyrs, who had sealed with their deaths the lives they had devoted to following Christ, strengthened our faith, conscious as we were that we had not yet persevered to the end. When we learned that there were still Hutterian Bruderhof communities in America, we contacted them and a lively correspondence followed. We had never had any desire to be a group on our own and had always sought unity with other movements and communities which were led by the Spirit. In 1930 Eberhard went to America and stayed almost a year with the Hutterians, visiting all their communities.

In spite of the fact that the Brothers, who had lived in community for four hundred years, had different views about some things, which were then and still are a matter for discussion between us, we decided to join with them, since they were closer to the early Christian Church than any other groups known to us at that time.

When Eberhard came back from America, an intensive time of spiritual and numerical growth was given to us. Many new people from Switzerland, England, Sweden, and Germany joined us, including some from various groups which were seeking unity just as we were. During this time people from the Werkhof near Zürich and from a community not far from Eisenach came to us. During the years that followed, other similar groups joined us.

We had some sharp disputes in our discussions with the guests in those days, because the spirit of National Socialism had begun to spread through Germany. When Hitler came to power in 1933 the progress of our work was stopped and we saw all the more clearly how hostile the spirit of National Socialism was to ours. The government issued restrictions which made our work in Germany increasingly difficult. In November 1933 the Bruderhof was taken over by the Gestapo, the S.S., and the police, and our school was closed. We were refused permission to receive guests and our social work and the sale of our books was made practically impossible. During the raid every member, in particular Eberhard, who was in bed with a broken leg, was exhaustively questioned. When the detachment left, they took with them a whole car full of books and papers which they confiscated.

We had been told that a State school with a Nazi teacher would be set up at the Bruderhof. We decided, therefore, to take the school children, about twenty in number, to Switzerland without delay. When the teacher came there were no children to be found. The young people over school age also went to Switzerland.

Eberhard and I went to look for a new place, which we found in the little principality of Liechtenstein next to Switzerland. Here we rented an empty summer hotel at Silum in the Alps at an elevation of nearly five thousand feet. This was a venture in faith since we had no money at all with which to fit out a new community. Help came though, just when we needed it most. In March 1934 the children and young people reached Liechtenstein by various routes. After several families had also come from the Rhön Bruderhof, we founded the Alm Bruderhof. During the months that followed, Eberhard and I made frequent trips back and forth between the two settlements, each time never knowing if we would return. Those were times of danger when many people were being arrested and thrown into concentration camps.

Germany was arming. In the spring of 1935 we were faced with the difficult question of whether the young men of the community who were eligible for military service should stay in Germany and witness against war and the spirit of militarism, or apply their energies to building up the new community in Liechtenstein. After some profound consideration by the whole Brotherhood we saw that our witness is not merely the rejection of war and injustice,

but to a much greater extent our life's work is
to build for peace. So the young men went to
the Alm Bruderhof which soon had grown to a
hundred people, children and adults. The number soon increased by an influx of new members
from England. Eberhard had made a trip to
Holland and England in the spring of 1935,
giving talks, and, incidentally, investigating the
possibility of a better location for settlement in
England in case the Alm should turn out to be
only a temporary home.

Only the Swiss, English, and Swedish members, with very few Germans, stayed in Germany
after that, and difficulties multiplied. In the
midst of this situation, when the community
was living in a state of inorganic separation
imposed from without by political conditions,
Eberhard had to submit to a surgical operation
on the advice of a medical friend. It was hoped
that the operation would help his broken leg
to heal. After this operation he died quite suddenly in the Elizabeth Hospital in Darmstadt
on November 22, 1935. To the last he bore
witness to the way and direction which must
be demonstrated to the whole world, today as
then: the brotherly life in peace and justice.

A few days before his death, Eberhard Arnold wrote the following:

"All Bruderhof members must be won for the greatness of our cause. We have still not arrived at a real missionary activity; it is becoming ever more urgent to ask for it.

"The most important thing of all is the faith in God's greatness, in the supercosmic significance of Jesus and the future of the universal Kingdom of the Spirit. This is the context in which repentance, forgiveness, faith, certainty, personal dedication, and all the rest belong, and nowhere else.

"From the standpoint of this greatness, we should always answer movements of the times without being infected by them.

"My heartfelt wish for our future is that the Bruderhof communities may never grow narrow and intolerant toward young people but should always help them to find a joyful new beginning of true life.

"God and His Kingdom are the most significant facts for everything that has significance. God and His will have such great meaning for everything that nothing else, no matter how great its significance, can stand comparison with it, and yet everything else finds its true meaning for the first time in this light. How small is the life of the individual in itself; how small the family life of a man, his wife, and their children; how small is the circle of friends bound to us by personal sympathy; and finally, how small is the whole Sparhof [former name of the Rhön Bruderhof] with all its little people. But how great are God and His Kingdom! How great is this historical hour of world crisis, world distress and world catastrophe; how much greater still is God's hour of judgment of the world and the Christ-hour of liberation that is coming! How burning our desire should be to know all these things more and more deeply and to share in them; how fervently we should expect and long for the day itself, the coming day that will bring freedom and unity!"

A PERSONAL WORD BY EBERHARD ARNOLD

Spoken on the occasion of his
fiftieth birthday, July 26, 1933

On this day I have been especially conscious
of my lack of ability and of how unsuited my
own nature is to the work I have been given,
remembering how God called me when I was
only sixteen years old and how I have stood
in His way, with the result that so much of
what God must have wanted to do by His
instruments has not been possible. It remains a
miracle that His work of the Church community
and the Holy Spirit is nevertheless revealed and
mightily testified to, in us feeble human beings—
not through our merits, but because we are ac-
cepted time and time again through the grace
of Jesus Christ and the forgiveness of sins.

I have had to think of the Shepherd of
Hermas, how he describes the building of the
great and mighty temple of marble, and how

he keeps referring to the many stones that must be thrown away. The attempt is made to fit them into the building, but if they cannot be used, even after their corners are chipped away by stern, sharp strokes of the chisel, then they must be thrown away—as far away as possible. But even the stones that are used must be chiselled very sharply before they fit and can be set into the wall. When we look back on the years that Emmy and I have been seeking, so that the Church community might be gathered—it is a miracle that we may still take part in it; this is only possible through an infinite Power—then we become very serious, thinking of the many people who for years have been intending to seek this way. I have received a list of all the friends who felt they were called to join us or believed in the necessity of entering into the work of our common life. A lot of these stones that seemed for a while to be possibilities have been thrown away again. That is very painful. It troubles and pains me to think of all these stones that have been thrown away and I wish the day might come when one or another of them would be taken up once more to be chiseled.

Another thing concerns me very much: the powerlessness of man, even of the man who has been entrusted with some task. Only God is mighty; we are completely powerless. Even for the work that has been given us, we are wholly without power. We cannot fit even one single stone into the Church community. We can provide no protection whatsoever for the community when it has been built up. We cannot even devote anything to the cause by our own power. We are completely without power. But I believe that just this is the only reason why God has called us for this service: we know we are powerless. It is very hard to give an account of or tell how it has come about that all of us, especially we older members of the Brotherhood, know we are so completely powerless. It is hard to describe how all our own power is stripped off us, how our own power has been dropped, dismantled, torn down, and put away. What I should wish for our younger Brotherhood members too is that this dismantling of their own power might be carried out to its full extent. That is not attained so easily and does not happen through a single heroic decision. It must be done in us by God. This is the root of grace: the dismantling of our own power. Only to the degree that all our own power is dismantled will God go on effecting the results of His Spirit and the construction of His cause through us, in us and among us— not otherwise. If a little power of our own were to rise up among us, the Spirit and authority of God would retreat in the same moment and to the corresponding degree. In my estimation that is the single most important insight with regard to the Kingdom of God. How it actually happens is hard to say. It is as hard to speak of this as it is to speak of the mystic Source of all things. The only thing that can be said is that the Holy Spirit produces effects that are deadly for the old life and that at the same time have a wakening and rousing power for the new life which comes from Christ and His Holy Spirit alone.

Let us use this day to give glory to God. Let us pledge to Him that all our own power will remain dismantled, and will keep on being dismantled among us. Let us pledge that the only thing that will count among us will be the power and authority of God in Jesus Christ through the Holy Spirit; that it will never again be we that count, but that God alone will rule and govern in Christ and the Holy Spirit. That means we declare our dependence upon grace. This is the testimony we are required to give. Everything we have is the unmerited gift of God. God can give this unmerited gift only to people in whom their own claims and special rights have been dismantled. And for this reason we acknowledge and ask for the grace that appeared in Jesus Christ and that comes to us in the Holy Spirit.

FROM LECTURES AND WRITINGS OF EBERHARD ARNOLD

THE CHARACTER OF LOVE

God's love is eternal and imperishable. It is the greatest and final revelation on our earth of God's universe. Greed and vanity, possession and property must perish because they are worthless for the eternal. Even the highest gifts of language, knowledge, and prophecy belong to time and will perish with it. Love, however, is simply life itself, life in every sense, full and everlasting life.

Hence the love that is *Agape*, in contrast to the intrinsically sick *Eros,* bears the character of Him who literally pours it out over us. It knows no bounds of space and time. It destroys nothing. It is the strength of unconquerable perseverance. It is steadfast faithfulness and therefore is equal to every task.

Agape, as genuine kindness, alone knows what is right for each person in every situation because it is free of the passionate stirring of naked Eros, which seeks by all the wiles of jealousy to win or to hold what it supposedly loves. It clothes the energy of our love in the divine light of inexpressible purity, which can never be unseemly or ugly and can never injure the modesty or sensitivity of the soul. Being God's love, it is free from all inflated arrogance, from all pretense, from all presumption for its own advantage.

Agape seeks and demands nothing for itself because it lives completely in the object of its love. It knows nothing of rights, for its nature is to abandon and forget the standpoint of rights, to find its happiness in giving. Vanity and envy are beneath it, therefore it can never be made harsh, never be thrown into excitement, never be provoked to bitterness. Agape sees the essential nature and potentialities of the other one; thus it does not take into account what may still be evil in him. Yet it has nothing to do with injustice. It concentrates its joy completely on the real, the genuine, the true in the soul of the other person.

Agape sees through everything which still delays the holy calling of a soul. It has the strength to be a protection, to endure and ward off all dangers that threaten to obstruct a person's destiny. It can do this because it is one with faith and hope, because it is completely in God, because it lives in the final fulfilment of man's future. For this reason alone, it is able to stand firm everywhere and to endure everything.

July 15, 1921

THE OLD CREATION AND THE NEW

The creation, overpoweringly mighty to the human eye, is the sublime spectacle in which God comes to meet the little heart of man. The childlike heart of the ancients never confuses God with nature. But the childlike man does not experience the might and greatness of God apart from nature. He cannot disregard the creation when he stands before the Creator. In the mysterious interconnections of the created worlds, the believing creature senses the might of the Creator who gives greatness, life, coherence, and unity to everything created. The man with a sense of awe feels an ultimate mystery in everything that lives. He grows aware that the living

creative Spirit must be greater than all created
life. Man stands amazed and awed before the
tree in the might of its life, before the living,
bubbling spring, beneath the life-giving rays of
sun and stars, and amid the fertility of the earth
and its life. Into a heart shaken and moved by
all this there falls the demand that above all
this mighty life, the great God of creation must
rule in undisputed power.

Innenland, p. 184

Whoever receives the Spirit of the new creation, which hastens on the end of all time,
receives the eternal powers of the one God, who
formed the first creation in the same spirit. The
future strength of God, in its all-transforming
expectation of the end, lives as the Spirit of
strength in the present aging creation. The new
dawn has begun in it already. Everyone must
see—a new creation is arising! Its Gospel is
meant for every creature.

Innenland, p. 383

This material world is a creation of the Spirit.
The cosmos is destined for the unity of spirit
and matter. The division that makes the spirit

struggle against matter and matter against the spirit is contrary to nature and opposed to the actual character of the creation. For this reason the time must come when the whole of matter stands in the service of God without the poisoning of life, without death the destroyer.

It was Jesus who asserted this ultimate and final affirmation of life in His mission. He proclaimed that Heaven and earth must become one. With this proclamation Jesus brings the true divine life down into practical, everyday existence. His concern is with daily and hourly life. His concern is the soul and hence the body as well.

The appointed task of man, since the primeval origin of his life, was considered to be the cultivation and keeping of the garden which had been given to him. But even the believing man of the Old Testament saw—the garden has not been kept; its cultivation has been disturbed by the Enemy who has sown weeds in it. The vigorous believer must rise all the higher out of the depth of this disappointment. The garden must be won back for God. God himself will conquer and rule it. But men must be ready to accept this rule of God. The Kingdom of God has the same earthly sound, the same earth-color, as the vanished Paradise. Sin, the destroyer, which has kept us from rejoicing fully in the earth, must be overcome. Not man, renewed by God, but the Enemy of God must leave the earth.

Jesus und der Zukunftsstaat, 1919

Let us pray fervently to God that our hearts, so moved now, might always keep finding new stimulation in the good thoughts that are God's, in the greatest facts; that we might think along the greatest lines, not in terms of continents or planets only, but in terms of the greatest stellar expanses; not merely in terms of the cycle of years, but in tens, hundreds, and thousands of years; in the dimensions of God's thoughts, in the great curves of God. That should be our prayer, such an earnest one, because the events of recent times have presented us with this special challenge.

Let us not be a petty generation under the impact of great things! Let us grow worthy of the fact that we have been entrusted with a great time and a great vocation.

Advent 1934

THE RULE OF THE SPIRIT

"Christ in you" is the secret of life in unity with God for him who is led through love from the death of isolation into the life of community. When God's Spirit dwells in us we are released from a life centered in and around ourselves, and born into a new life centered in and around God.

Freedom is redemption of the spirit, a call summoning a man away from his own lowly and ugly path, to be released and lifted up and away from the unspeakably hard struggle of the heart, the struggle between good and evil, spirit and flesh. We realize immediately that this freedom can never be produced by external measures. It can be brought into being only by the law of the Spirit and only when the Spirit of the Lord rules on the whole earth. Since Jesus came to the earth, since He died on the Cross and rose again from the grave, went to the Father and sent us His Spirit—since that time, the Kingdom of the Spirit has been present here in the midst of the country of man. We live in the country of man, and we do not want to leave this country of man as long as God would have us here. But

at the same time, we know we are citizens of a
foreign Kingdom, a Kingdom of the Spirit, and,
in the midst of the country of man, we represent
the holy interest of our Kingdom, to which we
belong in body, soul and spirit.

The beast in us must be governed, and the
beast in us fights against the rule of the Spirit.
The beast in us is not our final destiny. We can
sense that our higher destiny points toward the
Kingdom of the Spirit and longs for the rule
of the Spirit. We must stop and turn our eyes
inward so that the inner Kingdom can be built.
We must recognize the fact that freedom is not
the arbitrary whim of the isolated soul. Only
love is unity with eternal freedom.

Thoughts must become actions! It is time we
realized at last that thoughts are the giants,
and actions are their offspring. Fate is decided
in the world of our thoughts. In our aspirations
and reflections we decide matters of time and
eternity. Those that are in the flesh think of
things of the flesh, but those who are in the Spirit
think of the things of the Spirit.

As long as our mental life revolves about the
axis of our own ego, the magnetic attraction of
this ego draws us and holds us so that we cannot

be released; as long as we are bound to our own egotism we cannot be freed. Only when the soul can successfully be released from this thinking and brooding about itself is there freedom, freedom of the Spirit. "You have been dearly bought," the Spirit calls to us, "Do not become the slaves of men." If I wanted to please men I would not be the servant of Christ. The more we think about ourselves, the more we are committed to others. There is only one way to get free from slavery and that is the liberation from self. Freedom in the Spirit means freedom from oneself. This freedom has its life in God, in Christ. The mind of the Spirit is freedom, because its reflections are on God.

From lectures on the eighth chapter
of the Epistle to the Romans, 1918

PEACE AND JUSTICE

The grave guilt of those who have called themselves Christians is that they have restricted Christianity to the subjective question of the solitary redemption of the individual. That is the grandiose misunderstanding of the historical Jesus.
1921

There is no reconciliation with God without reconciliation with all men. There is no subjective Christianity in the sense of exclusive attention to one's own little individuality in its isolated relationship to its personal God, because there is no such thing as an isolated individuality, and God does not see a man out of the context of his relationship to other men. To become a Christian, to see God, to share in the Kingdom of God therefore means at the same time mercy to all; it means hunger, unquenchable thirst for a justice that includes everyone, for love that serves and for nonviolent dedication.

1921

When Jesus says, "Love God above all things," and adds that the other saying, "Love your neighbor as yourself," is equal to it, he expresses the fact that the social element is equal to the religious, and that the religious element, as people call it, is only then genuine if it is active in the social element.

October 18, 1933

Without justice there is no peace. Unless the earth's land is given back to the poor, justice remains lost on the stolen earth.

Peace belongs to all who do only good, in that they dedicate their all to love, and it belongs to them only.　　　　　　*Innenland,* p. 219

We know that even the discarding of armaments still could not mean a real state of peace in the world. We know that this would not mean the overcoming and abolition of hostility among men on this earth. Peace can mean only one thing: that all hostility is overcome, all hostile feelings stopped, all gaps bridged, all obstacles pushed aside, and all restrictions broken down. Where can such hostility be overcome? Where can the struggle of competition and the envious strife of business, and all hatred and envy, be overcome? We testify that these things can be overcome only in Christ.　　　　1917

When we speak of peace, we mean more than is commonly understood by peace of mind and the inner content and satisfaction of the individual. We certainly do believe that community with Christ also puts a man in unity with himself and within himself, whereas before he had been full of conflict. The will of God reveals itself as unity, down into the tiniest of worlds; but

the peace we mean goes further. It is God's will
to unity, which, from spiritual unity, brings all
relationships, all material things and all actions
into the unity of the Kingdom of God.

January 13, 1933

In all areas of personal and public life the
Church community must of necessity radiate the
peacemaking power of love, the power of Christ
who is alive within it.

1921

Unclean spirits are the really murderous spirits
that govern in the air. And if all wars were done
away with, pacifists would be forced to realize
that the spirit of murder is not done away with
so long as the atmosphere in which millions live
is filled with impurity. The same thing applies
to Mammon.

January 8, 1935

Because Jesus himself radiated in His nature
the organic unity of all the characteristics of the
coming Kingdom, no one can try to tear one of
the principles He announced out of its organic
framework and set it up as a law in itself. Whoever sets up pacifist work for peace, or purity
of heart, or any single moral or political demand

for itself alone, and demands and sets up the new cause from this standpoint, is on the wrong path. To be sure, without purity of heart, without active peacemaking, there can be no sharing in the Kingdom of God, but if the good tree is not planted the good fruit cannot be gathered. If the change does not extend to all areas, it is a lost cause to try to follow Christ's lead fervently in *one* principle.   1920

From Private Property to Community

The poisonous root of private property is disintegration, death and corruption. Private property arises through self-isolation, through the self-seeking of the covetous will. Private property brings a curse with it: there is a lack of relationship of individuals one to another and of the individual with God, who is the root of all life and being. Humanity lies in agony, on the verge of death, and the most obvious sign of its mortal sickness is private property.

Private property is the root of murder, the cause of war and the cut-throat competition of business life. Prostitution and marrying for money, which is no different, feed on it. It is the cause of dishonesty in business and of every kind of lie in human relationships.

"Business is business," men say, but when business is free to form a code of conduct peculiar to itself it means in fact that egotism and private property are framing an independent code. Our entire economy is based on greed, on the profit motive, or the individual's urge to self-preservation and his craving for greater power. Jesus once said: "If the kingdom of Satan were divided against itself, it would have fallen long ago." For this reason our highly developed capitalist economy does not fall, because the demonic forces let loose by greed and the profit motive work hand in glove with each other. They all follow the same line. The possessors thus become the possessed—possessed of demons. When one sphere of man's activity is permitted to frame its own laws irrespective of all other aspects of life, it becomes an idol, and man is ruled by demons. Life is rent apart and torn into shreds. That is the curse of our century, and we all fall down and worship such idols, especially where money and economics are concerned. Defending their collective egotism, men say: "I don't want my property for myself, I want it for my wife and children. I don't in the least want to go to war to protect my own personal property, but I'm going to fight for all." A man who loves wife and children loves his own flesh. Not only love for one's own family, but preservation of the clan, loyalty of tribesmen or settlers one to another, defense of nation or state, and still more civil war and war for one's own caste or class, is collective egotism.

Let me speak frankly: I oppose nationalism and patriotism; I oppose the class war of the proletariat; I oppose the class rule of the property owners; and in addition I oppose the laws of inheritance. I assert that egotism rears its head wherever there is any question of protecting common interests. I oppose the party system. The whole of our public life has fallen under this curse. Why are there armed forces? Why are there law courts? Why is there a militia? Undoubtedly they exist simply for the sake of property, that isolated thing which has become detached from all the rest, and which is doomed to death. We must break through this atmosphere of impending disaster. We are lost as long as the main factors in life are man's covetous will, his struggle for existence, his selfish claims and his selfish rights and privileges. We have fallen into a state of disintegration; we have fallen from God. This curse that lies over us, this ruined life, has become a commonplace fact that we take for granted. We must wake up and hear the Gospel which will free us from the curse of this life without spirit and without God.

Let us look at nature as a relief from these terrifying pictures. What maintains life in us, our natural life? We are kept alive by the sun, by air, by water, by the earth and its resources, by our own power to do strenuous physical and intellectual work and to take advantage of nature's potentialities.

To whom was the sun given? To everyone. It was given to *everyone*. If there is any one thing that men do have in common, it is this gift of sunlight. But there are men who live their life in the shadows. They must be brought out into the sunlight.

The old Hutterians say in their writings, "If the sun were not hung so high, it would long ago have been claimed by a few people as their private property, to the detriment of the rest who would then see nothing of it at all." The desire to own property, which takes for itself things which in no way belong to it, would not stop short at the sun. How is it with the air? The air is already in part a commercial proposition. Health resorts demand special charges, and so the air is bought and sold. And what of water? What of waterpower? What of the earth? Is there any reason why the earth should be parcelled out into private hands? Is the earth essentially different from the sun? No. Neither should the earth be private and personal property. The earth belongs to the men who live on it. God intended it for them, but today it is held by private individuals.

What is "private"? What does "private" mean? A private business, private car, private property, private road? *Privare* means to steal. Stolen property, then. Stolen from whom? From God and mankind, taken away from God's creation! The individual has taken hold of it for himself or has inherited it, which is the same thing, and each one holds fast to what he has. The fact that property is a curse ought to be plain to people on natural grounds alone, but there have to be prophetic spirits who put the facts quite clearly before men's eyes. God has always sent such prophets to men. Jesus is the

friend of man and therefore the enemy of private
property. Jesus wants men to have true life. He
attacks the urge to self-preservation as part and
parcel of egotism. One of Paul's letters tells us
that every man should be of the same mind as
Jesus. He did not cling to privilege. He gave up
everything. He took the lowest place among men.
He became not only the poorest but also the
lowest of men, for He was classed as a criminal.
He kept nothing back for Himself. He had no
money of His own: His wandering community
had a common purse. He said quite plainly:
those who obey the urge to self-preservation are
lost to life. He who would keep his life shall
lose it. He who does not leave all that he has
is not in harmony with me. No one who still
holds on to property is in harmony with Jesus.
Sell all that you have and give it away. Whoever
has more than one coat should give it away;
and if a man asks one hour of work from you,
give two—give your second hour away. The
second hour of work is otherwise the source of
private property. If all good gifts shall one day
belong to the whole, to God and His rule, just
as the sun does now and the earth will do in the
future, then assuredly your extra hour's work

belongs to God and to all people. Do not gather possessions. Let yourself be freed from all rights and privileges.

Even Nietzsche said that Jesus confronts the false life with a real life. What is the true life that we should lead? What is life? A body is alive when all the organs function as a conscious unit, cooperating with each other and enabling the body to do its work. Life is coherent unity in movement. Life is propagated by life, and only a living thing can give birth to new life. But life is inseparable from unity, unity of will, of feeling and of thought, and cannot exist apart from it. The living force within the individual depends on the extent to which humanity is united; and humanity is united only to the extent that it is led and directed by a collective soul, by the spirit of community, through which all support and work for all.

If we want community we must want the spirit of community. For this reason I reject the so-called Communist society. My faith rests solely in that society and commune that has faith in the Spirit. The collective soul of community is the Holy Spirit. In this Spirit the Church community is unanimous and united, is rich in gifts and powers and finds many ways of expressing the life that inspires it. We must remember, however, that just as the unity of the body cannot be maintained without sacrifice, so the unity of such a fellowship demands sacrifice if it is to be maintained. If this community could endure without any sacrifice on the part of its members, it would after all be nothing but the gratification of self-will. Every individual in the community must be prepared to sacrifice himself and all his powers, to dedicate his whole life.

This is true love: that a man lay down his life for his brothers. If we want to set to work in the Church community, we must have free, ready, and open hands. That is the only way to come into the fellowship, the only way to belong to the spirit of the Church community. If we grasp this mystery, we will understand that this message is the affirmation of life. It is no renunciation for the sake of renunciation, but liberation for the sake of new birth: liberation from illusion to win reality, an uprooting from the non-essential to reach the essential. Fire shall come upon this earth, the fire of holy torches, of beacon fires upon the hills, a network of organic living cells. All shall be united at the communal table, as guests at the wedding feast.

From a lecture in Vienna, 1929

THE WAY TO UNITY

Usually when people speak of interpersonal relationships they speak in terms of emotions, will and thought. Community is found in an emotional experience, or in exertion of the will toward the same objective, or, finally, in intellectual agreement.

We should like to point out an entirely different way, without meaning to depreciate or despise the three ways mentioned. As long as we are human beings we will have to use all three of them.

We say there is a completely different way that comprises everything real and essential in the other three and yet has an entirely different character.

If our dealings with one another in our group are limited to relationships on the horizontal plane, if we seek only the unity that is possible on *our* level, that is if we try to find unity and understanding only directly from man to man—

we can spend beautiful and inspiring hours together, there is no question of that. But the experience cannot leave us with anything fundamental because, like the clouds that drift about the earth, we are left suspended. We neither penetrate into the ultimate depth, nor are we really visited out of the ultimate height. The bond between us may not continue to be merely one from man to man. So long as we know each other only in this way we remain suspended: we do not take root and cannot really grow. But if the bond between us arises in the vertical plane, from the height down into the depth, and if we seek the bond in the vertical plane, from the depth up into the height, then the whole thing suddenly becomes different. Then we will see and know, taste and learn how these endeavors of will, these emotional experiences are subjected to the effects of a light and power that burns everything which cannot endure in the fire of eternal truth, and ignites everything that longs to be flame and light. Prayer and inward openness for true community rises upward like a flame. Our hearts have hands and arms of flame stretched upward to ask that this altar flame of sacrificial fire, this flame

So often, The power of love goes unobserved

[TORNADO = LIGHTENING POWERED]

of yearning and longing be fulfilled by the lightning from above, by the fire that comes from
heaven. The flame of longing from below toward
the height joins with the descending lightning
of the highest flame, and thus everything that
is sooty, smoky, and dark in our flame is puri-
fied. Because we find our first real fulfillment
in the flame from the other world, we can say
that it is not enough for us to find intellectual
agreement in our opinions, it is not enough to
realize that our wills are directed toward the
same objective, nor to realize a common, mu-
tual emotional experience in the currents of our
feelings. But we sense rather that something
else must come over to us to lift us off this
purely human level, to fill this human sphere,
this human level, with the powers of an entirely
different world. Just as the rays of the sun constantly stream on to our earth, as the lightning
brings light and fire down from the clouds above,
an element must burst into our midst which
does not originate from us. It does not come
even from our highest thoughts, endeavors, and
feelings, not even from the holiest part of our
being nor from our noblest special traits. It
really comes over us and cannot come from us.

Only through the Holy Spirit that comes over us is it possible to create a unit of consciousness that brings about a total agreement of all our thoughts, powers of will, and emotional experiences. Just as a person is a unit of consciousness in himself, the descent of this Spirit creates a unit of consciousness between those who receive it. The individual person means no more than a cell which belongs to the whole living organism of this one conscious unit of the Spirit.

March 18, 1932

THE CHURCH COMMUNITY

The Church community is a living building. The people in it are the living stones. These living stones have nothing perfect in themselves: they must be hewn and trimmed to fit better and better into the building. Yet the building is perfect. That is in fact the mystery of this building, that its life does not consist of its parts but of the living, all-comprehending Holy Spirit. It is not that the parts which have been collected represent the unity of the building— not the agreement of opinions. Through the fitting together of these stones, spiritually dead by nature, new life is aroused in them, not out of the various parts, but out of the all-comprehending, uniting element, the Holy Spirit.

July 30, 1933

Community can be compared with a loaf of bread. Seeds are scattered over many fields and farmlands. Then the harvest-time comes. The grain brought together into the granary is not always from one field alone. Often grain from many fields and farms is baked together in one loaf of bread. In the same way, the Church community is gathered together from many nations, many different strata of society, from diverse outlooks upon life, and is baked into one loaf.

May 1934

Where Christ rules, all political, social, and educational problems, all problems involving mankind as a whole are really solved. This realism of the original Christians is something that very few people today can comprehend. For this reason the words of Christ must be given body in the Church community. Because mere words about God's future get no farther than people's ears these days, some action must be taken, something must be created and shaped that no one can simply pass by. This is embodiment and physical reality. The primary element of this mystery is Christ. As Christ was in Mary, so He is in those who have faith and who love. The character of their attitude to life is the character of God's future. Through Christ, the Kingdom of the future takes shape now in the Church community. That is the reason why this Church lives in complete peace and justice. This is why it can shed no blood and tolerate no private property. This is why it cannot lie or take oaths. This is why it cannot tolerate the destruction of virginal purity, or of the marriage bond between two people in the community. This is also why it must be free of all conduct designed to magnify man.   August 3, 1934

The various nations maintain embassies in Paris, Rome, Berlin, and elsewhere. The ground on which the embassy building stands is inviolate. There no one can be subjected to the laws of the State in which the ambassador is living; on the embassy grounds, the only valid law is the law of the country which has dispatched the embassy. It is precisely the same with the embassy of Jesus Christ through the Holy Spirit of His Church community. The only valid law here is the law of life of the final Kingdom. Since the Church community of Christ has been charged with such a great embassy, its commission includes all men, without exception. It must reach all people. All men must come under the influence of the testimony to the truth that is the final goal of human history, this same unity of Christ which is shown in the embassy of the Church of Christ.

May 31, 1934

There is no lord in this Church community but Christ and Christ alone; there is no leader but the one single Head, who is Jesus Christ. We are all brothers together. We are all members, and we all serve. We are living cells. What governs in this Body through the power of the Holy Spirit is Jesus Christ, the Son of the Living God. The Son is the heart of God, and so Jesus Christ brings the most intimate element of the Omnipotent God. Where there is real Church community, He brings to expression the all-inclusive nature of Almighty God.

July 30, 1933

God does not work by only one method, paint in only one color, play in only one key, nor does He make only one star shine onto the earth. God's mystery is the rich spectrum of color that is gathered together in the purity of the sun's white light. The symphonic harmony of all the stars is built up on precisely their manifold variety. But all this is gathered together and will be gathered together at the end of time in the unity of the Kingdom of God.

May 1935

If community ceases to be here for all men, if it is no longer capable of concern for the distress of the whole world, then its life has lost its reason for existing. No man who puts up a real fight for purity, for community in his people, for pacifism, for the revival of the special character of his nation, or for any political ideal or social reform can do so merely from his own motivation.

May 1935

The mission of spreading the truth and gathering those who have been aroused is the task which has been given to the Church community from the very beginning. Groups must be sent out to work in homes and in the streets, to give brotherly help to all in need of food, clothes, and housing, to proclaim the coming Eternal Society. We believe that through our having been moved and shaken by forces out of the ultimate depths, there must come the inner authority without which our activity is meaningless and ineffective.

1929

FROM EBERHARD ARNOLD'S LETTERS

You know from the history of God's Church that there have often been such communities as ours, among the Moravian Brethren, in the Korntal, in the Baptizer communities and in those founded by Jean de Labadie, in Russia, Palestine, and other places. The essential consideration is not the economic form which the community idea has assumed. We are filled with the faith that the living Spirit of Christ is once more pressing toward the formation in our time of numerous small focal points, where there is not only the edifying community of a congregation, but real community of life, of productive work and vocation. It is to be taken for granted that the decisive question is the one of the people who form such a community. Certainly we shall have to endure many hard experiences. And

certainly not all who come to us will want to
stay permanently. But we are certain that among
those members of the Free German Youth Movement who have been gripped by Christ, among
working-class people who feel attracted by Him,
and among those in the German Student Christian Movement and the *Treubund* whom Christ
has set free, we have people in whom love
and the community spirit will overcome all
disturbing and hindering instincts.

April 27, 1920

You know that we envisage the structure of
our settlement in three work groups. The first
and actually basic cell of the settlement is the
agricultural group. The second group is com-
prised of the skilled trades of masons, carpen-
ters, and artisans. The third group consists of
people engaged in teaching, writing, and publishing, and other intellectual activity. It goes
without saying that the trade workers and those
in the publishing house and educational work
will want to work in the fields, too, as much as
possible. In times when everybody is needed we
shall lay everything aside and put ourselves
completely at the disposal of the farm as extra

hands. And vice versa, in slack times for the farm work the whole group can share in the current of our intellectual exchange. Many can be provided with a satisfying activity or a part-time occupation in this field.

June 9, 1920

A large part of the religious energy that has awakened in great sections of our youth is certainly to be attributed to Christ's working in secret. Therefore I regard this growth and development with joy and thankfulness. But another portion of it shows the work of demonic and pagan forces as well, and we must be on our guard. Hence it is always decisively significant to us to live for and testify openly to the unadulterated living Christ.

June 4, 1920

The task and mission of our periodical and our publishing house is to proclaim living renewal, to summon people to the actions of the Spirit of Christ, to spread the mind that was in Jesus in the national and social distress of the present day, to apply Christianity publicly, to testify to God's action in the history of our days.

It is not a Church question—it is a religious question. What we must do is to get down to the deepest life-forces of Christianity and to demonstrate that they are indispensable in the solution of crucial problems in contemporary culture. With breadth of vision, with energetic daring, our publishing house must steer its course right into the torrent of present-day thought. Its work in fields that are apparently religiously neutral is the very thing which will gain for us those relationships that will open new gates for our greatest tasks in life.   October 1920

Take courage! We must no longer see the little things. What is great must possess us so much that it engulfs and changes the small things.

I have courage and joy again for our life, though in the certainty that it will cost a great struggle, but a glorious one. The Spirit will be victorious over the flesh. The Spirit is stronger. It overpowers me, you, one after the other. This Spirit is compassion and independence, flexibility.

Our life will not grow narrower, but broader; not more confined, but boundless; not highly organized, but more fluid; not pedantic, but bolder; not more sober, but enthusiastic; not timid, but more daring; not more human, but more filled by God; not sadder, but happier; not more incapable, but more creative. All this is Jesus and His Spirit of freedom. He comes to us. So let us not be aggrieved by anything that has happened, but forget wherever others have offended us just as our offences need to be forgotten—and let us go into the future radiant with joy. Stay and wait until you are endued with power from on high.

Written from Holland after some had forsaken
the way of community life, July 20, 1922

How wonderfully the spirit of unity and the love of Christ and the power of the Holy Spirit have come to us again! May the Father, the Son, and the Spirit keep you and us in the unity of the Godhead. May His unchanging life and working lead you and us to steadiness and constancy, so that we remain in Him because He remains in us! How joyful and grateful we are for the wonderful leading and guidance of the Spirit in these past weeks! Now, through us, few and insignificant though we are, God holds two places for His testimony in active and

factual proof of His mission. We have suffered
defeats in the closing of the school, the discon-
tinuing of the orphans' home, the closing of
the community to guests, as well as our seriously
threatened economy. But in spite of the loss of
the children we loved so much, in spite of un-
settled economic questions, these defeats are now
not only made good, but as far as we can see
will be left far behind us after a few months
through a new spreading of the holy cause.
It is of course true that we must be ready for
more intense struggles. Our new beginning in
Liechtenstein, involving the necessity of seeking
help for our very existence, will have its inev-
itable consequences. Some effect must come
from the fact that growing circles in England,
Holland, America, Austria, and Switzerland are
becoming aware of the significance of true
Church community life. Men proposed to cut us
off so that we should have practically no influence on the world around us, but through these
events God has disposed that the wider world
takes more notice than ever before of what is
happening among us through God, and will go
on happening. It looks as though we are about
to enter a period when the community will

increase so much as to make all previous periods of growth small by comparison. More than this, a development of even greater significance for the history of our Brotherhood seems to be commencing, when the possibility and reality of true community life will find in many countries much more of the strong attention it deserves. It has been shown once again that it is not our care and anxiety, however loyally intended, that can provide the basis and continuance of our life, but only faith. This means, of course, that we must be all the more faithful in our stewardship and remain faithful stewards at all times.

After the founding of the Alm Bruderhof,
Easter 1934

LETTERS FROM FRIENDS
Recollections of Eberhard Arnold

It has been said of Hudson Taylor, the great missionary of the China Inland Mission, that as a child he was a "sensitive little boy" with a loving heart. The same applies to Eberhard Arnold's childhood. Our father called him fondly his "David," David being described in the Bible as being "ruddy, a lad with fine eyes, and a handsome appearance." We other four were all blond and blue-eyed. It was his big shining eyes that captivated his mother. He was an extremely courageous little fellow, staunch in enduring pain, with a great sense of humor and a happy enterprising spirit in our games outside in the garden or in the house in wintertime. Of course, I cannot say what was going on in the depths of his heart during these years of childhood. In our house, in which a strong and living fear of

God ruled, it was just not the custom to speak of one's religious life. I cannot recall that our parents ever gave us religious exhortations, and yet even in childhood the sense of being responsible to God for all our actions was deeply implanted in us. This we owe to the example of our father, whose whole being was actively infused by a profound fear of God and a holy reverence for the Bible as God's revelation.

But did not the very fact that God and His Word were taken so seriously lead inevitably to much unsatisfied longing?

Preconfirmation lessons and confirmation brought Eberhard nothing that could still the hunger of his spirit. But he had not long to wait until God met him in a way that surpassed all expectations. This was around the turn of the century. Germany was visited by God in a revival movement that brought streams of new life. Eberhard, who was just sixteen, spent his summer vacation in the country parsonage of his uncle Ernst Ferdinand Klein. Here, through the personality of his uncle and through some members of his congregation, who were Brandenburg peasants, he became acquainted with something quite new—a joyful victorious Christianity which had its roots in the certainty of the forgiveness of sins and of acceptance by God, a peace which remained inviolate through external suffering and struggle because it was simply a gift from above, and a joy in service of Him who had given His holy, pure, divine life for a mankind that had fallen into guilt and had constantly followed the wrong path.

Now came the great revolution in Eberhard's life. He had already recognized the sinfulness of his heart, which was no better than that of his comrades. Coming back to Breslau after his vacation, he arrived at a total and conscious dedication to his beloved Lord Christ in the service which he was given there in the Y.M.C.A. and later in the community. His whole life was immediately changed into a joyful service for Him. He told his teachers and classmates quite candidly about his conversion and ardently tried to win them for his Master. There was no one who was "safe" from him, whom he would not have confronted with the decision for Jesus. He struggled, alone and with other followers of Jesus, for souls that had still found no peace. Many years later, when the two of us met at a conference of the Student Christian Movement, he as secretary, I as student, he told me of the holy imperative which drove him from within to testify for Christ. That his whole heart was filled with the inner fire to serve in the love of Christ was already apparent, although not yet fully in his attitude toward possessions. With great loyalty to the will of God as he had recognized it, he bore all the difficulties and troubles that grew up in his way. Even in those days he never forgot the meekness and readiness to suffer which Christ demands in the Sermon on the Mount. From the very beginning of his discipleship his driving motive was to take all of Jesus' demands totally and seriously, and truly to continue the life of the first Church as described in the Acts of the Apostles.

Hamburg   HANNAH ARNOLD

My memories of Eberhard Arnold probably go back further than those of most people now alive. Our fathers were acquainted, and we knew each other as schoolboys in Breslau during the eighteen-nineties. I met Eberhard Arnold again as a university student in Breslau in the winter of 1903–1904 and once more in Halle in 1905–1906. If my memory is correct, it was in the summer term of 1906 that Eberhard Arnold took over the leadership of the Halle group of the German Student Christian Movement. In this period, as a pupil of Ludwig von Gerdtell, Eberhard Arnold was clear and firm in his devoutness in repentance, even aggressive toward the other students. But at the time of the First World War he gained increasing understanding for social problems. So it was that at the end of the war I felt he had an extremely close kinship to the Social Work-Community which I had founded in 1911. Eberhard Arnold visited me frequently in the East End of Berlin and in an executive committee meeting of the German Student Christian Movement I nominated him as editor of *Die Furche* ("The Furrow"), which Dr. Neidermayer and I had edited up to that time. Soon afterwards, Eberhard Arnold determined to found a community at Sannerz near Schlüchtern similar to our Social Work-Community. The basis of this community settlement had the full sympathy of the friends of the Social Work-Community. From then on his work developed further in the direction of the Bruderhof communities. After this, although I met him many times and kept up relationships with him in Liechtenstein during the years of my exile in Switzerland, in later years I saw very little of him. But we kept up a friendly correspondence till the last. I shared in his concerns and sensed profound joy in the fact that the Bruderhof cause was led through all troubles to a good goal. I can still see the worthy figure of my friend before me.

Dortmund   F. SIEGMUND-SCHULTZE

When I was elected to the executive committee of the German Student Christian Movement in 1917, while ex-Chancellor Georg Michaelis was president of the organization, I met Dr. Eberhard Arnold, then one of the S.C.M. secretaries, and worked in close contact with him especially in the literary field in the *Furche-Verlag*. It was he who started this publishing house which developed with great rapidity in connection with the prisoner-of-war service of the German Student Christian Movement. Even then he was the focus of lively discussion because he brought out publications in a much more modern form than that of similar Christian literature in Germany up to that time. Discussions became more vigorous and profound in the years after the First World War, with the appearance, among student groups and in the whole Youth Movement, of political currents tending to a strong separation to the right and to the left. The position, which he shared with some others in those days, led to an internal crisis in the German S.C.M. at the student conference in Oeynhausen in 1920. In the discussions, Eberhard Arnold took one side and Dr. Berg, the evangelist of later years, the other, with Hermann Schafft mediating skillfully between them. It must have been shortly after this that Eberhard Arnold left the staff of the German Student Christian Movement to devote himself entirely to the work in Sannerz and at the Bruderhof communities, in the course of which he found connections with the Hutterian Brothers in Canada. From that time on, I met him less often. But I remember vividly our last talk together during an excursion in Wilhelmshöhe; my memory retains the indelible image of a man in whom the flame of primitive Christianity burned, who sought in kindly humility and profound inwardness a way that cut across the most varied Christian directions.

Kassel-Wilhelmshöhe   D. ERICH STANGE

I first met Eberhard Arnold at the Christian student conference at Oeynhausen immediately after the First World War. The waves of excited debate were dashing high. Young ex-soldiers from Marburg spoke passionately against war and the capitalist state.

"We want to live. We have seen organized evil in action. We want to be the salt of the earth and let the ethics of Jesus flow undistorted into this confused age. Hence—no force, no killing, no taking of oaths, no serving as judge or policeman—but an embassy of Jesus to the sinful world." The radical ethic arises from experience of the grace of the Cross.

I took part in this conference more as a spectator until, through no intention of mine, I was drawn into the debate, which finally became an exchange between Eberhard Arnold and me.

I refused to accept the condemnation of the state and social order as "organized evil," and designated these structures as the result of the struggle between the invisible Kingdom of God and the equally invisible realm of evil. I maintained that the task of the Christian in this world of conflict between the two realms, was to struggle to give a more Christian form to existing institutions. But, I said, an immediate realization would not be possible for people active in politics.

At that time Arnold also did not advocate the absolute practice of the Sermon on the Mount in the literal, casuistic sense. The words of the Sermon on the Mount, he said, were to be understood as interpretations of the fundamental laws of the Kingdom of God and of the furthering of a life in the holy love of God. But Eberhard Arnold held to the position that certain concrete acts were impossible for him because they were obvious symptoms of sin. At this point the demands listed above came up again one by one.

Even then it became apparent that Eberhard Arnold was not trying to make a religious or ethical judgment of Christians whose professions lie in political or governmental life—for instance, chief of police. Rather he believed that his particular role was to point, through protest at these specific points, to the Kingdom of God for which we wait. The discussion in Oeynhausen, which was later continued in Saarow, Berlin, where Professor Heim entered into it, became rather complicated and cannot possibly be recounted here in brief. As long ago as that, the fundamental difference embodied in the different courses taken by the Habertshof and Sannerz was already clearly apparent.

These are two approaches to Christian existence which grant each other due recognition and which are distinct in their relationship to the State and to society. Both approaches refuse to follow Spengler or Naumann and let the antithesis of the Kingdom of God and the kingdom of this world continue to coexist unrelated. We cannot change the world as it is directly into the Body of Christ. Nowhere, not even in settlements of regenerated people, does the Kingdom of God already exist; and these settlements of such people can go on living undisturbed only because the power of the State protects them by force, police, and law from destructive onslaughts. Still, the experiment of a life like that developed by Eberhard Arnold or the Quakers is significant as a reference to something beyond itself. The "symbolic man," as we termed him in later discussions between the Habertshof and Sannerz, is significant because he points out the temporary nature of the existing social and political system. Hence his rejection of oaths, of military service, and so on. The "political man" on the other hand enters into the existing fabric of life, into the existing system of state and society, and tries to struggle and conduct himself within this system from the standpoint of the Spirit of Christ. In most cases perhaps this means a choice between two evils. But in no sense does it mean giving up the inward focus of endeavor towards the perfection of the Kingdom of God.

Each mode of Christian existence—such was the final understanding we reached—recognizes the other and each is aware of its particular danger. The political man is in danger of growing weary in his struggle to transform the world and of acting from tactical expediency rather than conscience. The symbolic man is in danger of a legal and pharisaical misunderstanding of his own distinctiveness as the uncompromising Christian existence, and of regarding the political man as a second-rate Christian. Each should realize that the other is a member of the Church, engaged in the same struggle, and stay clear of the danger of considering politically active Christians as dishonest compromisers, or accusing symbolic men of pharisaism.

Space does not permit the further illustration of this fundamental difference, say in the development of the respective legal shapes of the Habertshof and Sannerz, the former leading to a mutual-benefit cooperative, the latter to the "Bruderhof." But we ought to be ready to continue the discussion at any time if either feels it to be necessary or likely to be fruitful.

Kassel   HERMANN SCHAFFT

A decisive prelude to Eberhard Arnold's activity as publisher and writer was undoubtedly those years of his life which saw him acting as secretary of the German Student Christian Movement, and after 1916 as literary business manager of the Furche-Verlag which was founded in Berlin in that year. This was the work in which I, as sales manager and one of the founders of this publishing house, first met Eberhard. It is with especial pleasure that I recall those years in which he helped to lay the foundations of the Furche-Verlag, which later developed into such a large concern, and I am grateful for everything that Eberhard Arnold was to me at that time.

The first years of the work of this publishing

house were still under the sign of the First World War, and hence did not allow the true aspect of this new venture to be recognized. There was a change in the year and a half which remained for our work together after the war. Apart from his activities as chief editor of the monthly, *Die Furche* ("The Furrow"), in which his sister-in-law Else von Hollander was a loyal and valuable helper, and apart from all the lectures he gave in Berlin and on journeys, he also took an active part in shaping the new publishing house. Many of the approximately three hundred publications, which appeared under the imprint of the Furche-Verlag up to the time he left, owe their origin to his initiative, and their execution to his help. His direction seemed to give the authors wings. There are too many titles to recount them here. A circle of authors which was mentally alert and often very radical, especially in the post-war years, gathered around the new publishing work at that time. It was only later, when he was able to take up his own way unhindered in the work of the Bruderhof communities, that the thing he had conceived as the actual goal of his writing and publishing became reality.

My work and friendship with Eberhard

Arnold will remain with me as a spiritual possession, not to be lost as long as I live.

Berlin-Spandau   HEINRICH RENNEBACH,
Director of the *Furche-Verlag*

In the years 1919 and 1920, after the collapse of Germany, the Youth Movement, with its ideals of self-determination, individual responsibility and inner truthfulness, was the gathering point for many young people. They were those who believed in a renewal from within, and they came from every kind of political and religious persuasion. Among them was Eberhard Arnold, who appeared in my life for the first time when, early in 1920, he called members of the Movement to a meeting on the Inselberg in Thüringen, with the purpose of making Christian sources fruitful for this movement of renewal. He succeeded in gathering a group of friends with the desire to go deeper than the *Wandervogel*, who restricted themselves to the area of culture. This group consolidated under the name *Neuwerk*. We had celebrated Whitsun many times in the course of our lives. But that we should ever celebrate it with such ardor as we did during the Whitsuntide conference of the *Schlüchterner*

(as the *Neuwerk* group was called from the
name of the place where it met)—that was
something we would never have believed possible. We realized that our Christianity was
nothing compared with that of the primitive
Church.

What we all felt, Eberhard Arnold put into
practice, giving up his secure position in Berlin
to create a focal point of brotherly life with
communal property at the little farm at Sannerz.
In his work among students, he had seen how
many people did not find the way to the Church.
His settlement, where he went with his wife and
five children, was to be "an ever open door" for
the many people who were seeking a spiritual
home at that time.

I found out just how different the people were
who made their way there. For most of them, it
was only a station on the way to somewhere
else. Yet even these "guests" had the opportunity
to know what powers of love and discipline
radiate from a community whose members are
totally dedicated to Christ as the center of their
lives, and who devote themselves to each other
and to all people. Eberhard Arnold did not
think that all the *Neuwerk* people necessarily

had to follow him in giving up property and middle-class existence, but he was convinced that his vocation in our materialistic world was, with others, to give an example of such a communal life on the pattern of the early Christians.

In spite of the high ideals of the Youth Movement there was a great deal of moral confusion in it in those days. For instance, a section of opinion idealizing the inner bond of two people in love thought it right to dispense with all external bonds of marriage ceremony. On one occasion, a young man sat beside me when I was at Sannerz. I sensed his depression and asked Eberhard Arnold what was the matter with him. Eberhard told me he had had to give him a talking-to for holding such views, and added, "Where should we end up in Sannerz if we didn't take our guidance from the Holy Scripture?" Afterwards, I read this young man's entry in the guest book:

> I came as happy Johnny
> and left as sorry John.

I hope he thought it over!

Another time we were waited on at table by "Karlchen," an elderly man. He wore a white apron with a cook's cap on his head— a curiously refined service considering that the food was only stew in a bowl dished out with a tin spoon. Eberhard whispered to me, "Karlchen is a very willing and adroit 'gentleman of the road' who always comes to us in the winter. The white uniform has helped him to get rid of the dirt of his vagrant life." Karlchen was also the one who always urged the guests to leave punctually when they had decided to go—otherwise a weak point at Sannerz.

What happened with another wanderer, who arrived one Sunday afternoon in a very decrepit condition, showed us how each one who came was received and fitted into the community life according to his gifts. After supper Eberhard Arnold began, "We have a court singer from Berlin with us tonight, and have the privilege of hearing him." Before our astonished eyes the tramp stood up, washed and combed and wearing a new shirt, told us some of his experiences and sang and sang for almost two hours. Nobody would have left or dared to interrupt him, Eberhard least of all. A homeless man felt he was at home.

At a conference we asked Eberhard Arnold how he could be so tolerant toward all the various opinions, persuasions and religions, considering his radical affirmation of the Sermon on the Mount and the teachings of Jesus. What he answered has stayed with me for life and helped me many times.

He said: "You have only to go back far enough. In the ultimate depths, everything good and true that men have ever known, thought, or lived, comes from the one source of light. Our vocation is to make the way free for it."

Stuttgart   HEIDI DENZEL

Eberhard Arnold came into my district administration office in Fulda one day and told me of the wish of himself and some of his friends from the Sannerz settlement to acquire a neglected farm in the Rhön near Fulda. In answer to my inquiry he gave me some information about the *Neuwerk* movement. He said there had been a separation because of a fundamental difference of opinion—the others refused to recognize miracles as a basis of economic existence. That made me listen with lively interest and sympathy. I wanted to help him. It was not possible to obtain a loan from the savings bank immediately. But when he came again he told me he had received from a friend the sum needed for the purchase. Through a mortgage the district savings bank then provided the necessary means for developing the place.

The Rhön Bruderhof grew and flourished through the diligent work of its members. There were hard times, of course. Eberhard Arnold's trust in God was never disappointed.

I have often admired the consistency of the Bruderhof people's Christian attitude to life. On one occasion, two of them—one of whom was a giant with the strength of a bear—were coming through the woods with the week's wages for their workers, when they were set upon by masked figures. Remembering Jesus' teaching, they did not defend themselves, but let themselves be robbed.

Anyone could find refuge at the Bruderhof. Often shady characters came from the big cities. The constables had a hard time establishing at least some kind of registration with the local police station. No one was turned away. When the provincial governor from Kassel had come for a visit and was leaving, Eberhard Arnold said to him, "You were here today as a government official. I hope you will come again soon—as a brother."

Even though the Bruderhof was rather like a foreign body in the ten-century-old religious unity of Catholic Fulda, nevertheless, in the deepest sense, there was a close relationship with the Christian spirit which Eberhard Arnold embodied, as there is everywhere where people try to be true Christians.

The National-Socialist revolution destroyed Eberhard Arnold's work at the Rhön Bruderhof. But it goes on growing in other places, to the joy and blessing of many. Eberhard Arnold's unreserved trust in God and his faith in the miracle of divine goodness has led to victory, even in the hardest times and over the stoniest roads.

Schloss Neuenbürg   HEINRICH BARON VON GAGERN
                             District Administrator, retired

The picture of Eberhard Arnold remains in my memory as that of few other men. I can imagine his face before me as if I had seen him for the last time only yesterday. There must have been something extraordinary about him for I have known many thousands of people during my lifetime. This monastic, retiring man, with his family on their lonely island, had become a dear friend to strict Catholics. This was not only because of his great love for the Youth Movement, where he found frankness, honesty, and genuineness, it was also the makeup of his character, his deep faith in the substance of the Christian revelation as he saw it, his absolute radicalism in the very best sense of the word. One might tend to despise a man who would not take up the sword to bring about order in the world, but with Eberhard Arnold it was his Franciscan attitude which urged him to take this stand; his followers took the consequences upon themselves at the time when Hitler reintroduced conscription. It was the legacy which Eberhard Arnold left behind, living in their hearts. He also left it to me, the Catholic, and pointed out certain things which always, or almost always, came short or were overlooked by those representatives of the Church whom I had met up to that time. He counted me as one of his own, and I reckoned him as one of mine, as belonging to the Church that I love, the Church that knows no boundaries, where

he really belongs, even if legally he has no right
there.

Velbert/Rheinland   NIKOLAUS EHLEN

Our friends will be surprised that in this letter
I talk with you as if you were not beyond or
beneath, but right in the midst of us. I see you
laugh, my dear! What does the day know of
the "yonder" and the "beneath" and of the
"present?" What is known of how all this is
one and that nothing dies that has ever lived?
You belong to the few I have met who are genuinely alive, an original spontaneous individual.
I am thankful for this. You are dead? Oh, my
dear friend, they do not know the other side
of life, working more mightily than the presence
of the many, which when fulfilled shines into
the future. At this light more and more life is
kindled as it burns out of eternal life. You are
no "poor soul" in timid anguish. When I think
of you, you are present, close to me, because we
are not just you and I; no, we are alive from
one Spirit, even if we may call Him by different
names. You know, "In my Father's house are
many rooms" (John 14:2), but it is only *one*
Father and only *one* house.

So now we are together again, my dear, at

Sannerz, on the Bruderhof in the Rhön, in my study on the banks of the Neckar. Together we look at the world, at the people around us and at what urges or hinders them. As if it had only been today I still remember how, in the time of our periodical *Der Rufer zur Wende* ("The Caller to Change"), which is now nearly 30 years ago, I wrote to you whom I at that time did not know, from Binau on the Neckar to "Sannerz, post office Sterbfritz." Sterbfritz! This name makes me happy. How often on the way to you at Sannerz I passed through this Sterbfritz, a quiet village surrounded by meadows. We understood one another very quickly and when after years my son Tilmann was born, I asked you if, being your godson, he might also bear the name Eberhard.

When we were together, often long and by ourselves, at Sannerz and later on the Bruderhof near Neuhof in the Rhön, the people came and went, young and older ones, many, often strange, just as those times brought them to you. They looked for a refuge in their need which they could not master. They were wrapped up in themselves, unnatural, cramped and stiffened, exaggerated, without a binding task, and without the goal that points beyond oneself. They were without the goal that could unite them with the whole and with men who know it and love it. Your house had an open door and no one was first asked who he was. The answers would often have been strange.

You were publishing at that time a series of "Source Books," testimonies to the Spirit throughout the centuries. In our talks and gatherings we concerned ourselves with the expectation of the Messiah in religious writings outside the Bible, with the early Church, with Staupitz, Böhme, and Kierkegaard, with the mystery of history, with Goethe, and we sang together the songs of the Youth Movement and your *Sonnenlieder*.

A great deal was being done in the fields and in the house. Together we toiled for a right understanding of people and things around us. My dear Eberhard, I shall never forget the twinkle in your bright eyes, your amused smile with the cunning little beard, your cheerful laughter, when strange things or far too human things tried to press on us. When we were "fed up with the dryness" of it all we would meet it with humor, even with irony, not to despise, no, but to stimulate and to waken.

That was your uniqueness, my dear. Your witness was pithy, manly, free of the poisonous look of hypocrisy. You had no love for stuffiness, sweetness, or twaddle. There was no penetrating smell of "Christianity," no cliquishness, or sentimentality about you. To seek out heretics was just as foreign to you as was the addiction to straighten out everybody according to your own way. You valued other people as long as they were earnest, and you came to terms with the insincere. You also found a way with the most pigheaded peasant and with the most stubborn "man of God." You were a man and a brother to them, their neighbor, when they needed you. Your manner was at all times cheerful, genuinely animated by the trust that carries even into the nights. How often did we laugh heartily together, yes, we freed ourselves by laughing with a truly "Homeric laughter." I can still remember, my dear, when you told me how your father, a theology professor at the university, audibly recited a Hebrew text to himself applying the correct throat sounds and you children quietly listened and imitated him, about which he wasn't especially happy.

You lived life right from the center and out

of the depths, comprehensive and free. You did
not inherit Christ from others as one to whom
you got accustomed nor as one in whom you
excelled, but out of your own inner experience
and encounter. You were truly one who is freed
by Christ, who has been changed by Him. You
were free of anxiety. Your faith was no mere
acceptance of truths, no flight of fear. It was
certainty. It was on a world-wide foundation.
And therefore there was nothing of conventional
Christianity in you, which economically supports
a man and brings him advantages. You were
not impressed by men of pretentious faith. You
knew precisely that Christ was no "Christian."
You did not think much of the puffed-up mani-
festations and messages of a doubtful Christianity
nor were you seeking in it the salvation of the
"Occident." You saw right through it and its
impossibility of changing man, because you lived
the pure "kernel" of the good tidings which is
hard to live. You opposed all appearance and
pose and all self-righteousness. You were not
concerned with the dogmas about which theolo-
gians quarrel and which brought about the fall
of just some of the most earnest among them.
You went along with your great namesake,

Gottfried Arnold, and with his impartial *Church and Heretics History*. But, no, you were concerned wholly with the life of Christ, with the community of the brothers and sisters renewed and changed through Him in the sense of the primitive Church. What you wanted had grown in the clear consciousness of the knowledge of all learning. You took man as he is. You were as distant from illusion as from misunderstanding. You knew the demonic powers, the weight of the age—and which age would not be full of burden and need? This did not come to you as an isolated recognition, but as a binding call to help your brothers. You knew the binding power of the small Church community, especially in the great current of a completely different world. You never recruited. Whoever was called, heard, and thus they came to you; some to live with you and your friends in community; others, touched by the insight that something could happen that turns the need, were in harmony with you though they did not stand fully in the communal work. There are rings and circles that stand closely or more distantly around you, as the kernel, a guard and help to you.

How often, my dear Eberhard, was all of this,

were you, present in me as I wrote the poetry *Der Menschensohn* ("The Son of Man"). You, as only few did, understood this testimony of my experience in the encounter with the Son of Man, with Jesus. It is Jesus who appears as the bringer of good tidings from eternal life to the here and today, of the eternal life not only yonder, no, but here and today because He overcame the "world," through being reborn in the light of the Father. Here I know ourselves to be one. Once I was not able to reveal myself in poetry. But you would certainly have liked my *Hymnen an der Götter Griechenlands* ("Hymns to the Greek Gods"), for I wrote them close to you, as I wrote the "Son of Man." His character as God is also enlightened from "Hellas" in a unique way.

Let me embrace you, my dear! The blood of our love revives you. You are present. You are a witness of the new life apparent in Christ; a man of kindness, but also of such decisiveness that spirits are discerned and separated. A friend of freedom, a brother of knowing love.

Heidelberg-Ziegelhausen   HERMANN BUDDENSIEG

God is Bond.
Take the hand!
Unto God make firm your vow,
Make it now.

Close the ring!
Joyful sing.
Garlands of flowers take for the dance.
Radiance!

Spirit-gripped.
Move as one.
Circle round, circle round,
Center bound!

Stars in dance!
Light advance!
Hear the music of the spheres,
Heaven to our ears!

God is song,
Light—Sea—Throng:
Hear and see, hear and see
Harmony!

Gott ist Band
Sannerz, 1923

Twilight deepening, hope disappearing,
Temples crumbling, nothing binding:
The day departs.

Brooding clouds, heat oppressive,
Dark powers slinging lightning flashes:
The night awakes.

Glittering hollowness, grotesque vanity,
Envy, strife, and poisoned dullness:
The Serpent rules.

Hard, cold mankind! Bitter misery!
Through great burdens prayers pierce upwards.
The morning comes.

Glowing Light shines o'er the chaos,
And that Light redeems in judgment:
The Sun is ris'n.

Peace now smiles, joy purifies,
Spirit heals, Truth unites:
The day is here.

Poison yields, harsh chains fall,
Freedom binding—jubilation!
The Lord now reigns!

Dämm'rung flutet
Sannerz, 1923

Thou, Thou! Spirit of Christ, whate'er I've done,
I trust in Thee.

Thou, Thou, Risen One, art ever here,
I see Thee.

Thou, Thou! What am I? Whate'er I've been,
I rest in Thee!

Thou, Thou, Power of the World, Thou givest life.
I give Thee mine.

Thou, Thou, seest those who have betrayed Thee,
I love Thee.

Thou, Thou, Coming One! Thy Kingdom come:
I wait for Thee.

Du, Du! Jesus Geist
Sannerz, 1922

In silence surrounded,
Alone in the dawning,
New sparks joined together
In shared joy are forming.

Full wide are hearts opened,
The circles completed,
Men find one another
In new way united.

The members in rhythm
Swing, hands reaching out. For
The songs are now ringing
Renewal for all things.

Now hearts find each other
In purity holy.
The garlands are woven
In unity radiant.

> *In Stille versunken*
> Sannerz, May 1923

The Word anew revealed
Shines out with truth and light.
We view in deepest wonder
The Spirit's new-built house.

To truth awakened newly,
We wait to hear God's call:
And step by step He leads us
The way He longs for all.

His Way is newly opened,
His Kingdom comes so near.
His Message is all powerful:
Our Strengthener is here.

Das Wort uns neu geöffnet
Mark 3:13–15, Sannerz, 1921

We pledge the bond now.
The brothers hearken
Our watchword:

That peace prevail and
The earth shall be in
God's possession!

That every heart shall
From pangs of hell
Find freedom,

In steadfast unity,
In Spirit's purity,
Be brothers!

In joyful labor
The task glows brightly:
Work-oneness!

The world beholds it,
The bond will build it:
Spirit-Communion.

> *Der Bund beschwöre*
> Sannerz, 1922

God is the Unity
In holy purity;
Christ is the Love,
All hearts to move!

His is the mission,
Fulfillment giving
Those who as brothers
United are living.

We are the messengers
As He has commanded.
Each one a brother
To love one another.

So lives the unity
In holy community:
His love the power
To work in this hour.

Gott ist die Einheit
About 1929

On the original is written: "Out
of a heart full of thankfulness for
the renewed experience with you
faithful ones."